T0349207

THE ENGLISH BOROUGH

IN THE

TWELFTH CENTURY

THE ENGLISH BOROUGH

IN THE

TWELFTH CENTURY

BEING TWO LECTURES DELIVERED IN
THE EXAMINATION SCHOOLS OXFORD
ON 22 AND 29 OCTOBER 1913

BY

ADOLPHUS BALLARD

HON. M.A. (OXON.), B.A., LL.B. (LOND.)

TOWN CLERK OF WOODSTOCK

Author of *The Domesday Boroughs, The Domesday Inquest,
British Borough Charters* 1042—1216, *&c.*

Cambridge :

at the University Press

1914

CAMBRIDGE UNIVERSITY PRESS
Cambridge, New York, Melbourne, Madrid, Cape Town,
Singapore, São Paulo, Delhi, Tokyo, Mexico City

Cambridge University Press
The Edinburgh Building, Cambridge CB2 8RU, UK

Published in the United States of America by Cambridge University Press, New York

www.cambridge.org
Information on this title: www.cambridge.org/9780521237888

First published 1914
First paperback edition 2011

A catalogue record for this publication is available from the British Library

ISBN 978-0-521-23788-8 Paperback

CONTENTS

ABBREVIATIONS

B. B. C.   *British Borough Charters* 1042—1216.

E. H. R.   *English Historical Review.*

D. B.   *Domesday Book.*

THE ENGLISH BOROUGH IN THE
TWELFTH CENTURY

I. BURGESS AND LORD

THERE is no need for me to begin this lecture with a definition : the lawyers of the twelfth century applied the name of borough to certain places and gave the name of burgesses to their inhabitants; this they did to distinguish these places from their neighbours which were called manors; and in order to ascertain what were the characteristics of an English borough of the twelfth century, I propose to select the salient features of the 300 odd charters of a date prior to the death of King John which relate to the privileges and duties of the burgesses of the various boroughs. M. Petit Dutaillis objects to the use of the term borough, and thinks that "its misleading technical appearance has perhaps greatly contributed to plunge certain English scholars into blind alleys[1]" : but our examination will show that there were certain features in the boroughs which distinguish them

[1] *Studies Supplemental to Stubbs* 71.

from the unprivileged villages ; and I may be permitted to say that I have found myself hampered in dealing with French municipal charters by the lack of a technical term which would distinguish the privileged from the unprivileged towns : for it was not every privileged town that was a commune.   In the first of these two lectures I propose to deal with the borough from the point of view of the burgess and of the lord : and in the second to consider the place of the borough in the national organisation.

In the first place, the borough was a home of freedom : but freedom is a matter of comparison, and the position of the burgess must be compared with that of the villager. Of the two classes of villagers, the villeins were more or less servile in status ; their rents were mainly labour rents and a distinguishing mark of villenage was the liability to work on the lord's demesne for a certain number of days every week, and also at specially busy times such as ploughtime, haytime and harvest ; the villeins could not give their womenfolk in marriage without the payment of a fine for the license of the lord; they could not send their son to school without a similar payment ; a fine was due from them if they sold their cattle : if they sold their land such sale could be effected only by surrender of the land to the lord and the subsequent admission of the purchaser who often had to pay another fine on his admission: he was liable in many cases to be tallaged at the will of his lord; when he died his lord took his best beast by way of heriot, and his heir paid a heavy relief on succeeding to his father's land: if his heiress were unmarried, the lord had the right of giving her in marriage to whomsoever he chose, and he usually chose the highest bidder: all these restrictions reduced the villein to a state of economic slavery. The tenant in socage was better off: his rent was a money rent though he often had to work on his lord's demesne at specially busy seasons: he could sell his cattle and even his land without the payment of a fine to his lord: usually no heriot was payable on the death of a socager, and the relief, if any, was but nominal: his kinsmen were the guardians of his infant children and the lord had no control over the marriage of his heiress.

On the other hand the burgess held his lands by burgage tenure which was a peculiar form of socage tenure: his rent was a money rent, and except in a very few cases he was exempt from all liability to work on the lord's demesne. The burgesses of Leicester and Lancaster had redeemed their agricultural services before the end of the twelfth century but the burgess of Egremont was still liable to provide a man to plough and another to reap on his lord's demesne[1]. The distinguishing

[1] *B. B. C.* 94—5.

feature of burgage tenure was that the burgess was at liberty to sell his land and to go where he would[1], without in general the intervention of the lord or his steward; but this freedom was limited in three directions: there were some towns where a burgess might not sell his house which he had inherited, without first giving his kinsmen an opportunity to buy it at the same price as that which had been offered[2]: and this custom is also found in France and Germany[3]. At Whitby, the Abbot, who was lord of the town, had a similar right of pre-emption, and at Walsall the lord could purchase for 12*d.* less than any other person had offered[4]: but I cannot find any similar provision in any French or German charter. And the charters of many towns forbad the burgess to sell his burgage to men of religion or religious houses[5], and thus anticipated the statute of Mortmain. Coupled with this liberty to sell, was the privilege that the burgess could devise his burgage by will[6] and give his daughter in marriage without the consent of his lord[7], and occasionally he was allowed to appoint guardians of his infant children by his will[8].

Normally no heriot was payable on the death of

---

[1] *B. B. C.* 64—8.
[2] *B. B. C.* 69—70.
[3] *B. B. C.* cx, cxxiii.
[4] *B. B. C.* 69.
[5] *B. B. C.* 69.
[6] *B. B. C.* 73.
[7] *B. B. C.* 76.
[8] Pembroke *B. B. C.* 78.

a burgess and at Pembroke, Lostwithiel, Bideford, and Bradninch, the heir's relief was fixed at 12*d*.[1] Common to Great Britain and the greater part of North-western Europe was a clause which gave undisputed title to a burgess who had been in possession of his tenement for a year and a day[2]. There were, however, some towns where the burgess was bound to grind his corn at the lord's mill and bake his bread in the lord's oven[3], and no inconsiderable part of the lord's income was derived from these sources. The burgesses of the boroughs which were situate on the King's demesne, were, like the villeins, liable to be tallaged at will, and during the reign of Henry II such tallages or aids were levied every three or four years[4]; but at Egremont, the burgesses were liable for the three feudal aids, those for knighting the lord's eldest son, for marrying his eldest daughter and for ransoming his person; they were also liable to pay aids when his military tenants paid aids but all aids were to be assessed by the burgesses[5]. But what especially marked out the borough as the home of freedom was the privilege that a serf who resided there for a year and a day became a free man[6]: Dunwich, and the boroughs that had charters founded on that of Dunwich,

[1] *B. B. C.* 76. [2] *B. B. C.* 71, cx, cxxiii.
[3] *B. B. C.* 96. [4] *B. B. C.* lxxx.
[5] *B. B. C.* 91. [6] *B. B. C.* 103—5.

required his admission to the guild as well as his residence in the town, and the Egremont charter, which had been granted by Richard de Lacy, refused this privilege to villeins from the King's demesne : at Chesterfield, the lord had a veto on the admission of a new burgess[1], but we never find in Great Britain a clause which is very frequent in French charters, forbidding the admission to the franchise of the men of certain lords[2].

In the second place, the borough was a jurisdictional unit, that is to say, it had a court of its own with jurisdiction over all its inhabitants, except that in some of the larger towns, there were sokens belonging to certain magnates or churches where the burgesses were, in the first instance, justiciable in the courts of the sokens. Domesday book shows that many boroughs were hundreds of themselves and the borough court was frequently called the hundred. Of course in the thirteenth century, the manor was a jurisdictional unit, for the manor court had jurisdiction over all the inhabitants of the manor, but the position of the burgess in this respect was superior to that of the inhabitant of a manor in that, while the villagers could be summoned to the hundred and shire courts, most borough charters contained clauses exempting the burgesses from suits of hundreds and shires[3], or from pleading or being

[1] *B. B. C.* 110.   [2] *B. B. C.* cxii.   [3] *B. B. C.* 123.

impleaded elsewhere than at the courts of the borough[1]; but to this general exemption there were occasional exceptions, and eventually the rule came to be that pleas relating to lands situated or to debts contracted within the borough could be tried only in the borough court, while pleas relating to lands situate elsewhere and to those burgesses who were servants of the King could be tried elsewhere[2].

Edgar's law provided that the borough court should be held thrice a year, and the Whitby charter shows that there were three general pleas at which every burgess had to present himself under penalty of a fine[3], and that, when required, minor pleas were held to which any particular burgess could be summoned.

Naturally the law administered in the courts of the various boroughs cannot be reduced to a code, but it may be laid down as a general rule that borough law was usually archaic both in its procedure and its rules ; the old pre-conquest rules of compurgation were preserved in the boroughs long after they had given way to inquests by witnesses and jury in other courts : and our charters show that the number of compurgators varied from borough to borough, and that sometimes a borough required more or fewer compurgators according to the nature

[1] *B. B. C.* 115—121.   [2] London 1155. *B. B. C.* 116.
[3] *B. B. C.* 142.

of the offence[1]. The formal pleading of pre-conquest times was still required in the boroughs, except where there were provisions against miskenning, that is, against the rule which caused a party to lose his cause if he failed in the correct repetition of his formulae[2]. Two of the legal innovations of the Norman conquest were absent from the jurisprudence of the boroughs: they were quit of the murder fine, the fine imposed on a hundred or district in which a murder had been committed[3], and except at Pontefract and Leeds, they were exempt from trial by battle[4]; in this latter particular, the English burgesses differed from those in France, Germany, Spain and Palestine, where trial by battle was the general rule, and most elaborate provisions were laid down for the conduct of duels[5]: I have found only one French and three German charters exempting the burgesses from trial by battle, and at Beauvais the commune retained a hired champion at a fee of 20 sous a year[6].

One of the most highly valued privileges of the burgesses was their exemption from arbitrary fines[7];

---

[1] *B. B. C.* 137—9. For compurgation in the County Court see Maitland, *Const. Hist.* 205.

[2] *B. B. C.* 146.   [3] *B. B. C.* 150.

[4] *B. B. C.* 132—4.

[5] *B. B. C.* cxiii, cxxiv, cxxx, cxxxiii.

[6] *B. B. C.* cxiii.   [7] *B. B. C.* 151—7.

the charter of Henry I to London directs that no
one shall be amerced at more than his wergild, 100*s*.:
and there were many boroughs in which the limit
was fixed at 12*d*., the same as in the Norman bourg
of Breteuil ; in the Devonshire boroughs the limit
was usually 6*d*., while in his new borough at
Eynsham the Abbot fixed the maximum at 10*s*.   In
some of the Irish boroughs we find a distinction
between greater and lesser pleas ; in the greater
the fine could not exceed 5*s*. and in the lesser the
limit was 1*s*. ; the Egremont charter alone provided
a nicely regulated scale of fines, in which the lord
tried to make the punishment fit the crime, and in so
doing punished a burgess who insulted his male
neighbour by a fine of 3*s*., but reduced the fine to 4*d*.
if one woman insulted another, and in the latter case
the complainant, was also fined 4*d*. if she failed in
her cause.   In a few cases the amount of the fine was
fixed by the culprit's fellow burgesses.   It is in this
connection that we see one of the greatest differences
between English and French municipal charters, for
in France most charters contain a nicely regulated
scale of fines, far more elaborate than that of
Egremont : it is very rare to find a French charter
fixing a maximum limit for all offences with but one
or two exceptions, as is found so frequently on this
side of the channel[1].

[1] *B. B. C.* cxiii.

Three charters allowed private compositions for offences; the Norham charter says that free burgesses were wont to settle their offences privately, and implied that this rule prevailed in other towns also; at Whitby the prejudice in favour of these private compositions was such that it was not till after a man had made three attempts at a private settlement that he could summon the offender in the borough court[1]. It should be noticed that whereas that offenders convicted of any offence had to make payments both to the offended party and to the lord of the court, the Wells charter exempted the burgesses from any payment to the Bishop, the lord of the town, when they made these private settlements. Similarly, the men of Hythe and Dover were declared to be witefree, that is free from the wites payable to the lord of the borough court on conviction for offences[2].

Finally, from the point of view of the student of jurisprudence, the most remarkable of the jurisdictional privileges of the burgesses was the privilege that they had of distraining on the goods of their debtors from other towns, or on the goods of the neighbours of those debtors, in order to secure their appearance in the court of the borough[3]; but this privilege could not be exercised at certain times,

---

[1] *B. B. C.* 112—3.   [2] *B. B. C.* 182—3.
[3] *B. B. C.* 161—4.

especially on market days, and by the end of the twelfth century many charters forbad distraint on any person who was not the principal debtor or his surety, a prohibition which was made general by the Statute of Westminster in 1275. It is to be borne in mind that this privilege of distraint to secure appearance in the court of the borough is confined to the British Isles, and is unknown in contemporary French charters except at Rouen, which was part of the English dominions till 1204[1].

So far we have been discussing characteristics which are common both to the boroughs of the British Isles and to the privileged towns of the north-west of Europe: especially do the French charters appear to be directed towards securing the freedom of the burgesses—their exemption from feudal or seignorial exactions—and the privileges of their own law courts; but when we come to the next characteristic of the British Borough, we come to a characteristic which is more emphasised here than on the Continent. For thirdly, the English borough was a place of trade; our pre-conquest kings had again and again forbidden traffic outside of boroughs; Maitland suggests that there were two reasons for this prohibition, the prevention of trade in stolen cattle and the facilitation of the collection of tolls[2]; after the Conquest these rules were not

---

[1] *B. B. C.* cxiv. [2] *B. B. C.* lxvi.

repeated, but Henry I forbad all trading in Cam-
bridgeshire except at the borough of Cambridge[1],
and his grandson issued an order to the sheriff of
Lincolnshire requiring him to compel all foreign
merchants to take their wares to the city of Lincoln,
so that the reeves of the city should not lose the
royal customs[2].   In Scotland the old rules prevailed
much later than south of the Tweed : for William
the Lion, who did not die till 1214, forbad all trading in the counties of Aberdeen, Perth and Inverness
except in the three burghs of the same names[3]; but
there is no similar prohibition of trade in any Irish
charter nor in any Continental charter of which I
have any knowledge.   Although the charters are
sadly deficient in evidence on the subject of markets,
yet it may be presumed that most of our boroughs
had weekly markets and periodical fairs; there were,
however, markets and fairs in villages which were
not styled boroughs.   In some of the boroughs
the burgesses had the right of forming a merchant
guild[4], that is, of uniting all the traders of the
town into a society which passed bye-laws and
made regulations for the good behaviour of the
traders and the improvement of the trade of the

[1] *B. B. C.* 168.   [2] *Ib.*
[3] *B. B. C.* 169—170.   Eventually these rules would tend to
the protection of the burgess against the foreign trader.
[4] *B. B. C.* 202—7.

town: only members of these merchant guilds were at liberty to open shops in the town, and where there was no merchant guild the charters often forbad others than burgesses to carry on certain specified trades in the town[1]. One of the rules of these merchant guilds insisted that every guildsman must submit any dispute of his with a guild brother to the judgment of the guild, a rule that caused no loss to the lord in those boroughs where private composi- tions were allowed; hence we often find two tribunals within a town, the court of the merchant guild dealing with disputes between the members of the guild and presided over by the head of the guild, and the borough court dealing with other disputes and presided over by the bailiffs of the King or the lord : Mr Salter has clearly shown the two courts sitting side by side at Oxford[2]. In a few towns we find rules forbidding the keeping of taverns by others than burgesses[3]; and in Scotland a modifica- tion of this rule was pushed to extremities, for no tavern was allowed in the counties of Perth and Aberdeen, except in the towns of Perth and Aber- deen, and except in those villages where the lord was a knight and was actually resident.

But the most common of the mercantile privi- leges of the burgesses was their exemption from toll

[1] *B. B. C.* 211—4. [2] *Oxford Millenary Lectures*, p. 24.
[3] *B. B. C.* 216—7.

at markets and fairs; this privilege our kings
granted wholesale[1], and in many cases extended it to
their continental dominions and to Ireland; often
too it was granted by mesne lords over more
restricted areas[2]; the Earls of Cornwall exempted
the burgesses of the boroughs which they founded
from payment of toll within Cornwall, and Roger
de Lacy exempted the burgesses of Pontefract
from payment of tolls within the castellaries of
Pontefract and Clitheroe. Some of the royal
charters provided that in cases where toll had been
illegally taken from any burgess the sheriff of the
shire in which that borough was situate or the reeve
of the borough was empowered to retaliate by
seizing the goods of a person from the place where
the toll had been taken and detaining them till
compensation had been made to the aggrieved
party[3]; but this right must be carefully distinguished
from the right of the burgess to distrain on the
goods of his foreign debtor to secure his appearance
at court. Freedom from toll was not peculiar to
burgesses; our kings frequently granted this privilege to monasteries and churches and their tenants,
but no provision was ever made for retaliation in
case toll had been illegally taken from the churches
or their tenants. It is this exemption from toll which

---

[1] *B. B. C.* 180—190.   [2] *B. B. C.* 191—4.
[3] *B. B. C.* 195—6.

affords the greatest contrast between the French and English municipal charters of the twelfth century; in this country there were at least 40 boroughs whose burgesses during that century received from the king the privilege of being exempted from tolls throughout England; of the 65 French towns whose twelfth century charters I have examined not one received a grant of exemption from tolls throughout the dominions of the French king; but, on the other hand, a few favoured towns, such as Calais and Rouen, received from our English kings exemption from toll throughout their continental dominions. The absence of this privilege from French charters is possibly the result of the extreme subdivision of authority in that country, but it is tempting to suggest that its presence in English charters is evidence that our English kings and their advisers, even in those days, were supporters of an enlightened commercial policy, and anticipated Adam Smith in holding that the best way to encourage trade was to remove all restrictions on it.

A fourth characteristic of some English boroughs was that they were military strongholds, but the military importance of the towns is more prominent in France than in England during this century. We all know the part that the garrison theory has played in the discussions on the origin of the English borough, but it must be confessed that the charters of the twelfth century throw no light on this question ; the knights and rural sokemen of the Abbot were obliged to assist the burgesses in the repair of the walls of St Edmund's Bury[1], and thus it is shown that even at the end of the century, burhbot was being exacted from the landowners of Suffolk, but the charters of Wallingford and Maldon exempted the burgesses from castle work[2]. The burgesses of Inverness covenanted with King William that if he would make a rampart round the town they would maintain a good palisade thereon[3]. But apart from these four charters and a very vague reference to the fortification of Hereford[4], there is no reference in any of the 330 documents that I have collected to the walls of any city or borough or the duty of the burgesses in repairing them : and it is not till 1224 that we find any charters authorising the levy of tolls for purposes of murage. Domesday Book shows that in the eleventh century the boroughs sent contingents to the fyrd at the rate of one fully armed man for every five hides of their assessment[5]; even in the sixteenth century military service at this rate was due from some of our boroughs[6]; these contingents were much smaller

[1] *B. B. C.* 93.　　[2] *B. B. C.* 94.　　[3] *B. B. C.* 94.
[4] *B. B. C.* 222.　　[5] *Domesday Boroughs* 80.
[6] Cambridge 1333 ; *Cooper's Annals*.　Oxford 1523 ; *Oxford City Records* 43.

than those required from the French communes. The charters of some of the frontier boroughs in South Wales provided for expeditionary service on the part of their burgesses; at Pembroke and Swansea the burgesses were bound to accompany the lord on his raids provided that they could return the same night[1]; a similar provision is found in the charter of Lorris, a small town to the east of Paris, whose charter was the examplar of many others[2].

To sum up, the advantages of a burgess over a villager were, that he held his lands in the borough by a money rent, and was free from all the servile conditions of tenure, that he could sell his lands and devise them by his will, that he was justiciable in a court of which his fellow burgesses were the doomsmen, and was usually exempt from attending the hundred and shire courts; and that in many cases that he and his fellow burgesses possessed the monopoly of trading within the borough, and could prevent a stranger from opening a shop unless he made a heavy payment to the guild.

These being the advantages of the burgess, what, if any, were the corresponding advantages to the lord of the borough? For landlords have never been in the habit of managing their estates on philanthropic principles, and if the status of a burgess was freer than that of the villager, this was

[1] *B. B. C.* 89.   [2] *B. B. C.* cxi.

not for any sentimental preference in favour of liberty on the part of the lord, but because he gained from the freer area certain advantages in pounds, shillings and pence. Very frequently he would receive a good round sum in cash as consideration for his charter ; the burgesses of Pontefract gave 300 marks of silver for their charter[1], while Richard de Grenville was content with a payment of four marks as consideration for his grant of liberties to the burgesses of Bideford[2]. Much larger sums were paid for royal charters, and the citizens of London promised King John 3000 marks for his charter of 1199 ; but John knew that promises were not payments, and therefore delivered the charter to the Chief Justice " so that if they are willing to pay these 3000 marks they shall have their charter, but if not, they shall not have it[3]."

Apart from the advantage of a cash payment on the grant of the charter the lord's income was usually increased by the establishment of a borough on his land ; in the first place, as to-day, so in the twelfth century the towns were more thickly populated than the villages, and therefore, from corresponding areas, the boroughs produced higher rents ; the sites of some boroughs were marked out as building estates, at Burton-on-Trent the area of each burgage was fixed at 24 perches by 4, or a little over half an

[1] *B. B. C.* 239.   [2] *Ib.*   [3] *B. B. C.* lxxxiv.

acre[1]; at Stratford-on-Avon the plots were about a quarter of an acre in extent, but in each case the rent of 12*d.* a plot was obtained[2], whereas the money rent of agricultural land was only 4*d.* an acre, so that, then as now, it was lucrative for a landlord to grant land for building purposes. Other sources of income would be the receipts from the mill and oven, the profits of the court and the market tolls, all of which would vary with the number of burgesses in the borough. But in addition to these regular sources of income, the lord derived occasional sums by way of aid and tallage : the periodical sums which the king received by way of tallage from his boroughs were assessed on the individual burgesses by the itinerant justices, and formed a substantial part of his income ; the *Dialogus de Scaccario* tells that occasionally the burgesses offered a certain sum to the justices as the aid from their borough, and if this was accepted, they assessed themselves in such a manner as to raise the amount ; but such an offer was a voluntary matter ; " the common liability of the town is always the result of its own act and not that of the government[3]." The income derived from the regular sources, the rents, the mill and oven, the law courts and the markets, was collected

---

[1] *B. B. C.* 51.   [2] *B. B. C.* 48, 49.

[3] Hughes Crump and Johnson : *Dialogus de Scaccario*, p. 231 qu. *B. B. C.* lxxxii.

by the reeve, who was often a speculator who would undertake to pay the lord a fixed sum and would recoup himself and obtain a profit from the exactions he levied from the burgesses. The charters show that he often added to his receipts in other and less legitimate ways; Henry II ordered that the citizens of London should be quit of Year's gift and Scotale[1]; the former appears to have been a gift levied by the authorities on New Year's Day, a precedent for the Christmas box levied by the modern postman, while the Scotale was a drinking party to which the burgesses were invited by the reeve, who afterwards made them pay for the drink that they had consumed. In the early days of the thirteenth century the burgesses of Malmesbury promised to pay 30s. a year to the Abbot for the release of three scotales which they had been accustomed to attend[2].

Domesday Book shows us that even in the eleventh century speculators had begun to take leases of cities and boroughs and to pay fines for the privilege of taking these leases, and the burgesses of Northampton appear to have taken a lease of their town from the sheriff in that century[3]; after the conquest, the custom of leasing boroughs to speculators was continued and extended, and the burgesses especially objected to an outsider coming

[1] *B. B. C.* 84.   [2] *B. B. C.* 85.
[3] *B. B. C.* lxxv.

in and taking the borough over their heads: the Pontefract charter contained a covenant on the part of the lord that he would not let the town to an outsider if a burgess would give as good a rent as he was otherwise offered[1], and in 1163 the burgesses of Derby paid a fine of £40 to the King that William Asturcarius should not have a lease of their borough[2]. But the best way of keeping out the stranger was for the burgesses themselves to take the lease, and in order to secure the lease, they were willing to pay an increased rent or a large sum in cash by way of premium. Thus, at the beginning of the reign of Henry II the citizens of Lincoln took a lease of their city at a rent of £180, an increase of £40 on the rent which had been formerly paid by the sheriff[3]: and in 1189 the burgesses of Cambridge paid the King 100 marks of silver and one of gold as a premium for the lease of their borough at the accustomed rent[4]. But as a general rule, the charters granting the boroughs at farm merely put the body of burgesses in the place of the reeve and did not give them any rights over the soil of the borough; certain land at Newcastle had escheated, not to the burgesses, who had obtained a lease of the borough, but to the King who granted a lease of these escheats to the burgesses at an additional rent of 110s. 6d.[5]

[1] *B. B. C.* 236.   [2] *B. B. C.* lxxvi.
[3] *B. B. C.* lxxvii.   [4] *Ib.*   [5] *B. B. C.* 237.

On the other hand, the burgesses of Bristol received a special grant of the waste places within that borough[1], and Richard I gave to the burgesses of Colchester the customs of the water and the shores on each side, "ad perficiendam firmam nostram," to enable them to pay their rent[2]. While speaking of the rents paid from the boroughs, it is interesting to note, that, while Magna Charta enacted that hundreds, wapentakes and shires should be let to sheriffs at the ancient rents[3], no mention was made of the rents of cities and boroughs, and the King was therefore at liberty to increase them to the utmost sum that the burgesses or a speculator would pay. Along with the right to farm the borough the burgesses became entitled to appoint their own official to collect the rents and to preside in the borough court, and the Dublin charter expressly mentions the *prepositura*, the provostship, as one of the appurtenances which passed with the right to farm the city[4]. It is interesting to compare the English charters granting the boroughs at farm with some of the French charters which had the same effect; for in France the grant to the burgesses professed to be a grant of the Prévôté, the provostship, with all the rents and dues received by the Prévôt[5].

[1] *B. B. C.* 237.
[3] *B. B. C.* lxxvii.
[5] *B. B. C.* cxvii.
[2] *B. B. C.* 236.
[4] *B. B. C.* 231.

There were other than merely pecuniary advantages which the lord derived from his borough. In the first decade of the thirteenth century, William the Lion built a new castle at Ayr and founded a borough at the gates of the castle[1], but in so doing, his aim was not to establish an additional fortification so much as to furnish the garrison with a base of supply. Remember how Domesday tells us that "in the town where rests the body of St Edmund there are living fourscore men less five, who are bakers brewers tailors washermen shoemakers embroiderers cooks and stewards, and all these daily minister to the Saint and the Abbot and the brethren[2]." And the Scots King would try to attract to his new borough men who would serve the castellan and his soldiers with provisions and clothes and other stores. For a castellan would sometimes have rights of purveyance[3], rights of taking goods for the King's use at a low price, and also an unlimited credit, except in those cases where a few of our mesne charters specify a limit within which the lord or his bailiff must pay for the goods which he has obtained[4]: the limit in England and Ireland was 40 days, but in France the limit varies from 15 days to three months; I have not found a 40 day limit in any French charter[5]. A French

[1] *B. B. C.* 3.   [2] *D. B.* II, 372.   [3] *B. B. C.* 87.
[4] *B. B. C.* 87—9.   [5] *B. B. C.* cxi.

custom, not found on this side of the Channel, was the ban, the right of the lord to forbid the sale within the town of certain goods, usually wine, for a specified time, during which time the lord had the monopoly of that article[1]. Then again, in certain towns, the lord had the right of prise, which in John's Dublin charter is defined as the right to take from every ship laden with wine that entered the port, two casks, one from before the mast and the other from aft the mast, at a fixed price of 40s.[2] I have already referred to the military services of the burgesses, but one or two charters require a little further notice; the Egremont charter provides that in time of war the burgesses should furnish twelve armed men for the defence of the castle, in time of peace they were to accompany their lord or his steward when he took a distress or made a seizure in Coupland[3], and at all times they were to set watches at the gates; similar watching service was required of the burgesses of St Edmund's Bury and Corbridge[4], and the burgesses of Haverfordwest were to accompany their lord or his bailiff when he went to Parliament or to the army[5].

To sum up, a lord would establish a borough on his estate, because thereby he would increase his

[1] *B. B. C.* cxvi.   [2] *B. B. C.* 235.
[3] *B. B. C.* 92.   [4] *B. B. C.* 93.
[5] *B. B. C.* 92.

income from the rents and other profits of the borough, and he would have at his door tradesmen who would furnish supplies for his castle, and also retainers who would be of service to him in times of civil trouble.

Hitherto we have been dealing with the advantages accruing from the establishment of a borough, on the one hand to the burgess, on the other to the lord: but we have not exhausted the differences between borough and village. Maitland begins his second Ford lecture with these words: "The borough community is corporate: the village community is not: this is a real and important difference —in the fifteenth century it shows out in clear light[1]." Granted, but although the difference between corporate boroughs and unincorporate villages is clear in the fifteenth century, it is scarcely visible in the twelfth.

Now, when we speak of the borough community as a corporate body, we mean that in the eyes of the law the individual burgesses lose their identity in a person that has rights and duties of its own, different from the rights and duties of each individual burgess. In the eyes of the law every person has a name of his own, can use a seal of his own, can possess property, can enter into contracts and can sue and be sued. Domesday Book personifies

[1] *Township and Borough* 18.

certain institutions but appears to deny personality to others: it represents the shire, the wapentake, and the hundred as having eyes and ears and voice, and as capable of taking and giving evidence: but the vill and the borough are never represented as giving evidence[1]. The whole of the controversy whether the burgesses of the eleventh century possessed corporate property would have been avoided if the Domesday scribe had personified the borough. But, as Maitland says, when we come to the fifteenth century, the difference appears clearly. The little borough of Woodstock received its first charter in 1453 and by it the burgesses were incorporated: they were declared to be one body in name and deed: and this body was empowered to use a common seal and was given the capacity to sue and be sued: and it received property in the shape of a certain meadow called Le Pool, and a grant of the borough at fee farm and also two fairs with the right to appropriate the tolls. But the burgesses of many boroughs acted as corporate bodies and exercised one or another of these functions long before they received a charter of Incorporation. Although the burgesses of Oxford were not formally incorporated till the charter of James I in 1605[2], yet they made corporate contracts[3], owned corporate property

---

[1] *B. B. C.* xcv.　　[2] *Royal Letters addressed to Oxford* 228.
[3] *B. B. C.* ci.

and used a common seal within the first quarter of
the thirteenth century. And when the text-books
speak of boroughs by prescription, they mean that
the burgesses have acted as a body corporate in one
or another of these ways without any formal incorporation. It must be remembered that many of the
boroughs which were established by seignorial grant
never attained the possession of corporate property
or a common seal, and never entered into corporate
contracts, although, as at Darlington, the borough
court made regulations concerning the trade of
the town, and authorised the formation of trade
companies. Hence we must distinguish between
corporate boroughs and boroughs which were un-
incorporated.

It is in connection with their property and
money that the burgesses first begin to perceive
the difference between that which belonged to the
individual and that which belonged to the body of
burgesses: in 1188 a charter was granted to the
burgesses of Preston granting them the toll of the
wapentake of Amounderness[1], and the pasture of
the forest called Fillewood[2], that is, pasture rights
in the forest: but while it was possible for the individual burgess to send his cattle to enjoy the pasture,
it is impossible to imagine that the charter authorised
each individual burgess to go on a free-booting

---

[1] *B. B. C.* 176.　　　　[2] *B. B. C.* 59.

expedition into the wapentake to collect his share
of the tolls : the burgesses must have appointed an
officer to collect the tolls and pay them into a common purse. Apparently, the earliest grant of this
kind is that contained in Archbishop Thurstan's
charter to the burgesses of Beverley about 1130[1],
when he granted them for eight marks a year the
toll of Beverley except at three fairs. It is not
astonishing that the Archbishop should have made
a gift to a body of burgesses and should have
thought of that body as a person, for often a monastic or collegiate church was personified to such
an extent as to be represented as the owner of
property : this idea is very prominent in Domesday,
especially in the south-western counties ; it was the
Church of St Peter of Rome that owned Periton in
Somerset[2].

But the most important gift that the burgesses
could receive was the grant of the borough at fee
farm, and before the death of King John 28 English
boroughs were held by their burgesses at fee farm :
but although the liability of the burgesses was joint
and several[3], that is, although the King's officer
might distrain on any one of the burgesses for the
whole of the farm, yet no burgess considered himself
entitled to a share of the income ; the collection of

[1] *B. B. C.* 176.　　　　　　　[2] *D. B.* I, 91 *a* 2.
[3] *Township and Borough* 77.

the dues and rents was the duty of one or more officers. Let us see what happened at Ipswich on the grant of a charter that the burgesses should have the borough at farm : immediately the charter arrived in the town, the burgesses met and elected their bailiffs and coroners, the officials sanctioned by the charter, a few days later they elected 12 capital portmen, and, after another interval, the bailiffs, coroners and portmen decreed that all the customs of the town should be collected by the bailiffs and four good men of the town, who were to pay the King's farm : and on the same day they ordered a common seal to be made[1]. Here it is evident that the grant of the borough to the burgesses at farm did not put a single penny into the pockets of a single burgess except the bailiffs, who collected the income and paid the rent and, as nothing is said on the matter, probably appropriated any surplus for their own use. As Maitland has pointed out, the charter authorised the burgesses to elect a bailiff to "run the town." In the fifteenth century it was held that the grant of a vill in fee farm to the men of that vill, incorporated the latter and authorised them to act as a body corporate[2]. That being so we have to deal with many incorporated

---

[1] *Gild Merchant* II, 119.

[2] *Y.B.* 7 Edw. IV, No. 7, qu. Pike, *Y. B.* 16 Edw. III, pt I, p. lxviii.

villages; for King John granted many vills, not styled boroughs, at farm to the men of those vills to whom he denied the style of burgesses.

I have been trying by this mass of details to present some idea of the usual burgensic duties and privileges in the twelfth century; but it must not be thought that this is a fair picture of medieval town life; Mrs Green has painted that picture once and for all, and I fear that my long details about the borough court and the law followed therein may lead you to think that the medieval burgess spent his time in nothing else but either suing his neighbour or being sued by him: but the charters and the custumals were drawn up by lawyers, and as the shoemaker thinks there is nothing like leather, so the lawyer thinks there is nothing like law, and especially legal procedure: if shopkeepers had drawn up the charters, we should probably have learnt more of the trading privileges of the burgesses. But the picture that I have tried to present is a composite picture, and the details are drawn from all parts of the British Isles. Two features, and two features only, can with certainty be predicated of every borough of the twelfth century, the application of burgage tenure to all tenements within its borders, and the possession of a law court with jurisdiction over all the inhabitants of these tenements.

2. BOROUGH AND HUNDRED

I finished my last lecture by stating that two features, and two features only, could with certainty be predicated of the English borough of the twelfth century, that all its tenements were held by burgage tenure, and that it had a court with jurisdiction over all its inhabitants. But this statement, which is apparently so simple, opens great difficulties when we come to consider the place of the borough in the national organisation.

For when we ask ourselves, what is the nature of the borough court, we find ourselves involved in a discussion as to the differences between feudal and royal or national justice. Maitland defines feudal justice as that justice which is exercised by one man over another because they stand in the relation of landlord and tenant[1], and the records of the thirteenth century show that then every lord was holding a court for the tenants of his manor; I do not know of any direct evidence for the existence of manorial courts in the twelfth century, but Domesday Book shows that there were then many men who were exercising over their tenants the rights known as sake and soke, a term which was used by the lawyers of the thirteenth century to imply the ordinary feudal

[1] *Domesday Book and Beyond* 80.

jurisdiction exercised by the lord of a manor over his tenants : it is therefore not unreasonable to believe that these owners of sake and soke held manorial courts in the eleventh century and *a fortiori* that there were manorial courts in the twelfth century[1].

Now the twelfth and thirteenth centuries were especially the age of the establishment of boroughs: we can compile a list of 26 English boroughs which were founded on their own estates by others than the King before the death of King John : sometimes the founders obtained the King's licence for so doing[2], but usually there is no evidence of such licence. One of the most pregnant examples of such borough-founding is to be seen in a little village about six miles from Oxford: for in 1215 the Abbot of Eynsham granted a charter by which he established a new borough in his manor of Eynsham : he cut out of the manor a piece of land about 20 acres in extent, which he divided into building plots: these

[1] Here I follow Prof. Vinogradoff, " As a rule the grants of sake and soke led to the formation of separate manorial courts " (*English Society in the 11th Century* 117—8), rather than Maitland, " It seems clear that when Domesday Book was compiled, and even at the beginning of the 12th century, sake and soke, whatever they meant, meant a jurisdiction that was not involved in the mere possession of a *manerium*." (*Sel. Pleas in Manorial Courts* I, xxiii.)

[2] *B. B. C.* I.

he granted to various tenants at a money rent[1], with powers of sale[2] and devise[3], *i.e.* on burgage tenure, and for the piece of land thus cut out of his manor, he established a court of which the burgesses were the doomsmen[4]. Now it is obvious that, as lord of the manor of Eynsham, the Abbot could ordain that the court of that manor should sit in two sessions, one for the inhabitants of the borough and the other for the inhabitants of the rest of the manor; and that being so, the court of the borough of Eynsham was a feudal court, a court wherein the Abbot exercised over the burgesses the rights defined by the term sake and soke. Long before the establishment of the borough, the Abbey had received a charter exempting its tenants from suit of shires and hundred moots, but even so, his justice was feudal in being restricted to his tenants in his manors and boroughs. There are many instances in which it can be shown that boroughs were formed by the separation of certain areas from the jurisdiction of the manors in which they were geographically situate, and establishing for them separate courts[5], and if, as frequently happened during the thirteenth century, a whole vill was raised to the status of a borough by a seignorial grant that it

---

[1] *B. B. C.* 45.   [2] *B. B. C.* 68.
[3] *B. B. C.* 74.   [4] *B. B. C.* 157.
[5] *B. B. C.* xci.

should be a free borough, the court for that vill would change its name but not its nature : in spite of its name being changed from Court of the Manor to Portmote, it was still feudal and would exercise no higher justice than it had previously exercised. And the contrary is also true : if a seignorial borough lost its burghal status, it reverted to the status of a manor : the new borough at Eynsham lost its burghal status long before the Reformation, and is to-day known as the manor of Newland, and its court to-day is the court of the manor of Newland. In fact, the sole difference between a seignorial borough and a manor was that the former was inhabited by free men holding on burgage tenure, while on an ordinary manor much land was held in villenage by men of servile status.

But feudal justice must be contrasted with national justice[1] : as soon as justice begins to be organised in this country, we find national courts for districts known as hundreds and shires ; and Edgar's law relating to the holding of moots implies that there were certain boroughs that had moots which were units in the national system of moots, and were co-ordinate with the hundred moots[2]. But in very early years our kings began to grant hundreds

[1] Much of what follows was inspired by Miss Bateson's criticisms of my *Domesday Boroughs* (20 *E. H. R.* 146).

[2] *Select Charters* 71.

to their favourite bishops and abbots[1], and with
the grant of the hundreds, that is, the grant of
the right to receive the dues paid to the hundred,
the grantees received the right of holding the hundred courts, and although these hundred courts were
in the hands of subjects, they did not become feudal
courts, for the relationship between the grantee of
the hundred and the landowners within the hundred
was not that of landlord and tenant : the effect of
the grant was to appoint the grantee as the King's
delegate for the holding of a national court with the
right to receive for himself the fees and perquisites
arising from that court. The thirteenth century
accounts of the Manor of Woodstock show that the
bailiff of the manor was in the habit of leasing the
hundred of Wootton to persons who paid a fixed
rent for it : in 1246 the rent was reduced from £12
to £11. 10s. "because it was diminished on account
of many liberties," and in 1271 he was unable to let
it, and therefore received the dues and accounted
for them to the King[2] : but neither the lessee nor
the bailiff was ever regarded as the landlord of the
suitors of the court.

We were speaking of the co-ordination of the
courts of certain boroughs with those of the hundreds as being units in the national system of courts ;

[1] *Domesday Book and Beyond* 267.

[2] *Woodstock Manor in the Thirteenth Century.*

and Domesday gives abundant evidence of such co-ordination. Every student of Domesday knows that, except in the south-western counties and Oxford-shire, it was the custom of the Domesday scribes to place at the top of the statistics relating to any manor or vill, the name of the hundred in which it was situate, except when the manor or vill under discussion was in the same hundred as its pre-decessor. Now when we examine the statistics of the boroughs in Domesday Book in relation to these hundredal rubrics, we find that they fall into three classes: the first class have no hundredal rubrics and therefore are outside the ordinary hundredal organisation: a second class lay in hundreds bearing their own names, while the third class, like Eynsham in the thirteenth century, lay in manors which them-selves lay in the ordinary rural hundreds. When we remember the effect of Edgar's law, we see that the reason why some boroughs had no hundredal rubrics was that they had moots which were co-ordinate with the moots of the rural hundreds, and were therefore equivalent to urban hundreds: if we look at the boroughs which lay in hundreds bearing the same name as themselves, we find that in some cases these hundreds contained no vills other than the boroughs, or that, in two cases, there were rural hundreds bearing the same name as the boroughs, but excluding the boroughs; so that these boroughs, too, may be considered as urban hundreds : for the sake of brevity, I propose to give the name of hundredal boroughs to those which are shown by Domesday to lie outside the ordinary organisation of the rural hundreds, and of them I count 46[1]. Their existence cannot be over-emphasised : the rural hundreds came up to the boundaries of the land belonging to these towns and there stopped short : five rural hundreds touched the boundaries of the borough of Cambridge ; and the boundaries of Leicester and Chichester were each touched by three rural hundreds : and it would seem that from the earliest days of the English settlement many of the old Roman towns had lain outside the ordinary rural organisation, but there is no evidence of the survival of Roman municipal institutions[2]. The moots of these hundredal boroughs were, according to Edgar's law, to be held thrice a year[3] : but these three sessions were thus particularised because to them alone all the burgesses were bound to pay suit without a special summons : other meetings of the borough court were held from time to time to which any burgess whose attendance was required was specially summoned.

Maitland adopts another classification of the boroughs of Domesday Book ; he notices that some

---

[1] For lists of various kinds of boroughs see note on pp. 44—5.
[2] See Appendix II.   [3] *Select Charters* 71.

are entered on the Terra Regis, and others lie on the land of some subject or another, while others, and these the most important, are placed above the line, that is, before the list of tenants in chief in any county, and are not stated to lie on the land of either the King or any other person[1]. I think that the key to this classification is the destination of the third penny[2]: Dr Round has pointed out that Domesday Book shows that in the time of King Edward the income of certain boroughs was divided between the King and the Earl of the shire in which that borough was situate in the proportion of two to one, and that the Earl's share was known as the third penny[3]. But, although this was the rule T. R. E., it was altered by the Conqueror; in some cases, where no earl was appointed, as in Wilts and Somerset, the sheriff accounted to the King for the Earl's third penny as well as for his original share, and in these cases the borough was entered in the Terra Regis: in other cases, such as Fordwich and Sandwich, the Earl had granted his third penny to the same person as had received a grant of the King's share, and these boroughs were entered among the lands of the grantees: while those boroughs whose income was still divided

---

[1] *Domesday Book and Beyond* 176—8.

[2] *Domesday Boroughs* 41—3.

[3] *Geoffrey de Mandeville* 287.

between the King and the Earl, were entered above
the line, and above the line were also found a
number of those boroughs about whose third penny
we have no information, but which gave their name
to the shires in which they were situate. None of
the boroughs above the line have any hundredal
rubric. Domesday mentions the third penny of 37
boroughs[1], to which can be added from other evidence, the names of two more[2], and of this total of
39, no less than 25 are included among the hundredal boroughs.

Another classification adopted by Maitland was
the division of the boroughs of Domesday Book
into those of homogeneous tenure, in which all the
burgesses held of one and the same lord, and those
of heterogeneous tenure, where different burgesses
paid their rents to different lords[3]; as three syllables
are shorter than nine, I suggest that we should
apply the term "composite" to the boroughs of
heterogeneous tenure; I can count 64 of these composite boroughs, and of them 43 are hundredal, and
five are definitely stated to lie within one rural
hundred or another: there are only three of our
hundredal boroughs which are not composite, and

[1] See note on pp. 44—5.

[2] Bedford, *Monasticon* IV, 414; Cambridge, *Cooper's Annals*
I, 38.

[3] *Domesday Book and Beyond* 197 etc.

before the conquest the Earl received the third
penny of these three[1].

These composite boroughs will repay a more
careful study, for examination shows that the
burgesses who held of others than the King or
the lord of the borough held their houses of the
rural landowners in the shire : except that where
a borough lay on the borders of two shires, landowners on both sides of the border held houses in
the borough ; moreover, these town houses were
appurtenant to, and paid rent to, and were often
conveyed along with the rural manors of these landowners[2].   The only evidence from which we can
deduce the duties of the burgesses who held these
appurtenant houses is the Domesday entry relating
to the city of Oxford[3], where there were 223 mural
mansions, which were so called because " if need be
and the King command, they repair the wall " :
now, of these 223 mural mansions, six were stated to
be appurtenant to four manors in Oxon. and Bucks.,
20 which then belonged to the King had previously
belonged to Earl Alfgar, who had been a rural
landowner, 189 belonged to 27 men who owned
land in Oxfordshire, leaving a balance of nine houses
belonging to six men who cannot be identified as

[1] See note on pp. 44—5.
[2] *Domesday Boroughs* 29, 107.
[3] *D. B.* I, 154 *a* I.

rural landowners in the county : so that of the mural mansions in Oxford, 96 per cent. were appurtenances of rural manors. Surely we are justified in deducing from these figures the rule that, in Oxford at all events, many of the rural landowners performed their burhbot by keeping houses in the city and burgesses in these houses to repair the wall. And as Domesday Book neither gives nor suggests any other explanation of the duties of the town houses which were appurtenant to rural manors, it is argued that in other boroughs too the duty of repairing the wall devolved on the town houses of the rural landowners, or the occupiers of such houses. If this be so, all our 64 composite boroughs were fortified towns at some time or another of their existence, for it is no part of the garrison theory, as I understand it, to argue that, at the time of the Conquest, these town houses were in all cases liable for the repair of the walls[1].

Possibly it will be interesting to compare this list of 64 composite boroughs with two other lists of fortified towns of an earlier date : from the Chronicle a list can be compiled of about a score of boroughs established by Edward the Elder to secure his conquests in the Midlands : of these, only nine retained their burghal status at the time of Domesday, but all nine are included among the composite

[1] See App. I. For Malmesbury see 21 *E. H. R.* 98, 722.

boroughs[1]. From about the same date comes a document known as the Burghal Hidage[2] containing a list of 31 boroughs, with the hidage of the districts which owed burhbot to each of them : of these, two[3] cannot be identified : eight had lost their burghal status at the time of Domesday[4], three are found among the boroughs of homogeneous tenure[5], and 18 are composite boroughs, one of which, Buckingham, appears also in the list of Edwardian boroughs[6]. So that, of some half-hundred towns which are known to have been fortified in the first quarter of the tenth century, 21 had fallen to the status of villages 150 years later, and 26 were composite boroughs ; but from their analogy with Oxford we have argued that the composite boroughs were originally fortified boroughs ; our enquiries therefore corroborate this argument in 26 cases.

A fourth characteristic is emphasised by those

[1] Buckingham, Chester, Hertford, Huntingdon, Maldon, Stafford, Tamworth, Warwick, Worcester.

[2] *Domesday Book and Beyond* 502—6.

[3] Heorepeburan, Sceaftelege.

[4] Burpham, Porchester, Tisbury, Bredy, Halwell, Watchet, Lyng, Eashing.

[5] Twineham, Lidford, Axbridge.

[6] Barnstaple, Bath, Buckingham, Chichester, Cricklade, Exeter, Hastings, Langport, Lewes, Malmesbury, Oxford, Shaftesbury, Southampton, Southwark, Wallingford, Wareham, Wilton, Winchester.

who attribute much importance to the existence of a
mint in a borough as evidence that the borough was
a place of trade ; but it is remarkable that the
situation of many of the early mint-stows affords
evidence in favour of the garrison theory ; and
shows that the towns were fortified before they were
places of trade. The mints of Alfred[1] and Edward
the Elder[2], and the earlier royal mints, were all
situate in the old Roman towns which became
English boroughs : Athelstan was the first to go
outside this circle, and of the 19 new mints established by him, five were placed in boroughs mentioned in the Burghal Hidage[3] and seven in places
fortified by Edward the Elder[4], while six others
were established in boroughs that contained houses
paying rents to rural manors[5]: in other words, 12
out of Athelstan's 19 new mints were established
in places which to our certain knowledge were

[1] Bath, Canterbury, Exeter, Gloucester, London, Lincoln,
Winchester (11 *E. H. R.* 759). Mr Stainer does not consider
that the OHSNAFORDA coins came from an Oxford mint.
(*Oxford Silver Pennies* xxxiii.)

[2] Bath, Canterbury, Lincoln, Winchester. (11 *E. H. R.* 759.)

[3] Wareham, Shaftesbury, Langport, Oxford, Wallingford. (*Ib.*)

[4] Weardburh (i.e. Warburton near Chester (Plummer, *A. S.
Chron.*), not Warborough, Oxon.), Tamworth, Warwick, Chester,
Hertford, Stafford, Maldon. (*Ib.*)

[5] Shrewsbury, Derby, Nottingham, Norwich, Dover, Hereford.
(*Ib.*)

fortified during the previous reign. Later kings multiplied mints with the result that of our 46 hundredal boroughs, no less than 40 contained pre-Conquest mints, and of our 64 composite boroughs 52 were mint-stows.

All of these characteristics, hundredality, the third penny, tenurial heterogeneity and the mint, point to the same conclusion, the national character of the boroughs possessing them ; the hundredal boroughs formed units in the national organisation co-ordinate with the rural hundreds and shires ; the third penny proves that the income derived from them formed part of the national income and was divided between the King and the chief official of the shire ; their tenurial heterogeneity shows that they were the national fortresses, and that their walls were repaired by residents who held their houses of the rural landowners ; the mints show that they were places of national trade. Any borough possessing any one of these characteristics naturally stands on a higher plane than its neighbour which possesses none of them : and it must therefore be noticed that all four characteristics are possessed by 22 boroughs, that three of them are possessed by 22, that two are possessed by 22, and that there are only seven which possess only one or another of them[1].

[1] 1. *Hundredal, Composite, Third Penny, pre-Conquest Mint.*
Cambridge, Chester, Chichester, Derby, Dover, Exeter,

Hereford, Huntingdon, Ipswich, Leicester, Lewes, Lincoln, Malmesbury, Norwich, Oxford, Sandwich, Shrewsbury, Stafford, Southwark, Thetford, Winchcombe, Worcester. (22)

2. *Hundredal, Composite, pre-Conquest Mint.*

Buckingham, Canterbury, Colchester, Dorchester, Gloucester, Hertford, Maldon, Nottingham, Rochester, Shaftesbury, Southampton, Stamford, Wallingford, Warwick, Wareham, York. (16)

3. *Hundredal, Third Penny, pre-Conquest Mint.*
Bedford, Torksey. (2)

4. *Hundredal, Third Penny.*
Fordwich. (1)

5. *Hundredal, Composite.*
Arundel, Bridport, Grantham, Northampton, Pevensey. (5)

6. *Composite, Third Penny, pre-Conquest Mint.*
Bruton, Bath, Ilchester, Langport. (4)

7. *Composite, pre-Conquest Mint.*
Bristol, Guildford, Hastings, Hythe, London, Romney, Sudbury, Tamworth, Wilton, Winchester. (10)

8. *Composite, Third Penny.*
Barnstaple, Cricklade, Droitwich, Milborne Port. (4)

9. *Third Penny, pre-Conquest Mint.*
Totnes, Salisbury. (2)

10. *Composite.*
Calne, Dunwich, Wimbourne. (3)

11. *Third Penny.*
Axbridge, Frome, Marlborough, Yarmouth. (4)

The Hundredal Boroughs are found in lists 1, 2, 3, 4, 5.

The Composite Boroughs are found in lists 1, 2, 5, 6, 7, 8, 10.

The Boroughs whose third penny is recorded are found in lists 1, 3, 4, 6, 8, 9, 11.

The Boroughs with pre-Conquest mints are found in lists 1, 2, 3, 6, 7, 9.

Every student of Domesday knows the capricious manner in which facts are inserted or omitted by the Domesday scribes : we have already noticed that the hundredal rubric is always omitted in the South-western shires, and it is therefore possible that certain boroughs in Devon, Somerset and Wilts, whose third penny, tenurial heterogeneity and mints are recorded, were also hundredal boroughs, and should be added to our list of boroughs possessing the four characteristics. In fact, I should be inclined to suggest that all the boroughs possessing one or another of these characteristics, 73 in number, should be placed in the same category, were it not that five of them, Yarmouth, Dunwich, Hythe, Romney, and Guildford, were definitely stated to lie within certain rural hundreds. But, although this conclusion is too sweeping, the fact remains that there were at the Norman Conquest and for at least a century and a half previously, a considerable number of boroughs that formed units in the scheme of national organisation : their courts were national courts, and their income was collected by the sheriff in the same way as he collected the rest of the national income, except in those cases where a hundredal borough had been granted to a subject. But in the same way as, when a rural hundred had been granted to a subject, that subject held the court of the hundred not as landlord but as the King's delegate, so, in passing to a subject, the court of the hundredal borough did not cease to be a national court. Every argument points to the conclusion that our oldest boroughs were always royal or national boroughs, units in the national organisation, like the rural hundreds and shires.

This digression into the character of the boroughs at and before the Norman Conquest may seem a side issue : but it shows that at the beginning of the twelfth century certain boroughs were more highly organised than their neighbours : and this distinction appears all through the century. The Pipe Rolls show that there were certain boroughs that paid a special tax, called indifferently an aid or a gift or a tallage : thus, the aid of 1130 was paid by 22 boroughs, of which 20 were included among the hundredal boroughs of Domesday : but additions were continually being made to the list of aid-paying boroughs, and the aid of 1176 was paid by 32 hundredal boroughs and 32 non-hundredal boroughs, but of the latter, six were composite in 1086, five paid the third penny and four were of homogeneous tenure.

The judicial reforms of Henry II however greatly affected the boroughs : the Assize of Clarendon provided that inquiry should be made for notorious criminals, who were to be presented to the Justices in Eyre by four lawful men of each vill and

12 lawful men from each hundred[1]. But the Assize makes no mention of presentments from the boroughs, and this omission is probably intentional as so many boroughs were urban hundreds, and it is implied that presentments from the boroughs would be made by 12 lawful men. Hence it is not surprising that when the shire was summoned to meet the Justices in Eyre, the sheriff was directed to summon 12 lawful men from every borough and the reeve and four lawful men from every vill[2].

From this time forth, a new criterion arises, a place which did not send twelve men to the Eyre was no borough, and this was probably the criterion which was adopted by the sheriffs in 1316, when they were ordered to make returns showing the names of the hundreds boroughs and vills in their respective shires, and the names of the owners of each : and when this return, known as the *Nomina Villarum*, is examined it is found that a number of boroughs are returned as being outside the rural hundreds, that others are returned as being within one hundred or another, and that the names are omitted of many that had received charters recognising their burghal status. Further examination shows that, except in Devon and Cornwall, the sheriffs omitted those boroughs which had received

[1] *Sel. Ch.* 143.
[2] Holdsworth, *Hist. Eng. Law* I, 440.

only seignorial charters, and usually returned the hundredal boroughs of Domesday as being outside the rural hundreds. Then, we learn that certain places, which had been hundredal boroughs in the eleventh century, such as Buckingham and Winchcombe, had in the fourteenth century ceased to be recognised as boroughs : that others, such as Yarmouth and Dunwich, had been promoted from intra-hundredal to hundredal rank : that others, which had formerly been assessed with rural manors, such as Reading and Steyning, had been granted hundredal rank, which had also been conferred on a few unchartered boroughs on the King's demesnes, such as Woodstock and Henley. It is, however, permissible to doubt whether there was any practical difference between those boroughs which were recorded as being hundreds of themselves and those which had separate representation within the hundred : so long as a borough was separately represented at the Eyre, there appears no reason, other than tradition, why it should be put in one class rather than the other. The twelfth century charters suggest that there were two methods by which a borough might be raised to hundredal rank : the burgesses of Portsmouth had been exempted from suits of hundreds, and Wells and Bridgewater had received royal grants of the " liber burgus," and all three towns were returned as boroughs in the *Nomina Villarum*, presumably because they were reckoned as hundreds and therefore sent 12 lawful men to the Eyre. It therefore appears that a royal grant of the liber burgus exempted its recipients from suits of hundreds and imposed on them the duty of sending 12 men to the Eyre : but a seignorial grant of the liber burgus had not this effect[1]. But these suggestions are tentative, and when the charters of the thirteenth century have been examined as carefully as those of the twelfth, it may be possible to decide definitely the reasons which led the sheriffs to call on certain boroughs to send 12 burgesses to the Eyre and to allow others to be unrepresented.

Two results of the *Nomina Villarum* may be noted : it seems to have settled the list of Parliamentary boroughs : previously these lists were so variable as to suggest that the sheriffs granted or refused Parliamentary representation at their own will ; but after 1316, with certain exceptions, of which the most are in Devon, Wilts, and Yorks, only those boroughs which were returned as such in the *Nomina Villarum*, sent burgesses to Parliament. It also appears to have settled the list of boroughs that paid the special taxation : for in 1322, Parliament granted the King a subsidy of one-tenth from the baronage and shires and one-sixth from the

[1] See App. III.

boroughs : with but a few exceptions, only the boroughs mentioned in the return paid the sixth : thus the seignorial boroughs of Burton-on-Trent, Leek and Walsall were omitted from the return and paid the tenth ; but the hundredal borough of Stafford paid the sixth : but in Devon a number of seignorial boroughs, which are mentioned in the *Nomina Villarum*, paid the sixth.

The co-ordination of borough and hundred appears in later centuries ; when the sheriff of Oxfordshire in 1635 received the writ for Ship-money, he issued his precepts for the collection of their respective quotas to the mayors of the boroughs and high constables of the hundreds in the county ; and it is remarkable that even in the sanitary legislation of the nineteenth century, the same co-ordination is observed. Under the Public Health Act, 1875, the whole country was divided between Urban and Rural Sanitary Authorities ; the Local Government Act, 1894, has changed the names of these authorities to Urban and Rural District Councils, but the districts over which the Rural District Councils exercise their authority are, in general, the Poor Law Unions established in 1834, and these Poor Law Unions are, generally, the ancient hundreds that had existed from the tenth century or earlier, or unions of those hundreds : so that for purposes of Public Health the hundred and the town are co-ordinate authorities. Of course, there have been many changes of area since the tenth century, but such changes are, comparatively speaking, very slight, and for our purpose, may be neglected.

To sum up, Domesday Book shows that in the eleventh century there were certain boroughs which were units in the scheme of national organisation like the rural hundreds and shires : this number was increased during the twelfth century by royal charters, and on all boroughs thus constituted, both new and old, the Assize of Clarendon imposed the duty of sending twelve burgesses to the Eyre as their representatives ; in the thirteenth century their separate representation at the Eyre was as definite a mark of the national importance of certain boroughs as was their position outside the rural hundreds at the time of the Conquest, and the co-ordination of hundred and town is to be found even at the present day. But one distinction must be borne in mind : the burgesses of some seignorial boroughs, like Eynsham, were likewise exempt from attending the hundred courts, but this exemption was extended to them, not because they were burgesses of a certain borough, but because they were tenants of a certain lord; and an exemption from the court of the hundred granted to a lord for all his men had not the effect of changing a seignorial borough into a national borough with its 12 representatives at the Eyre.

In many of the boroughs, however, which possessed national courts, co-ordinate with those of the rural hundreds, were to be found feudal courts exercising jurisdiction over the sokens that were situate within the boundaries of the borough ; when a landowner, who had sake and soke over his rural estates, owned houses within a borough, Domesday shows that he had sake and soke over his town houses also[1]; and in most, if not all, of our Cathedral cities, the bishop had sake and soke over that quarter of the city in which were situate the Cathedral Church and Close and the houses of himself and the Cathedral dignitaries. London is the special home of these sokens, of which there were at least 19 in the reign of Edward II[2], and some of these can be identified with the London houses which were appurtenant to certain rural manors at the time of Domesday ; thus, while Domesday speaks of 17 burgesses in London who paid rent to the manor of Lambeth[3], a conveyance of 1198 purports to grant one moiety of the manor of Lambeth and one moiety of the soken within London appurtenant thereto[4]. Kemble prints a copy of the writ by which the Confessor signified to the

[1] *Domesday Boroughs* 48.   [2] *Hundred Rolls* I, 401, 420.
[3] *D. B.* I, 34 *a* 2.   [4] *Monasticon* I, 177.

portreeve and bishop and burgesses of London his
will that the Abbot of Chertsey should be worthy of
his sake and soke over his haws within London and
over his own men[1], his haws being the town houses
which were appurtenant to his rural manors; and
Stephen ordained that the men of the soken of
St Peter of Westminster should be exempt from
attending the folkmoot and husting of London[2]. It
would seem from the London custumals and from
the writ relating to the soken of St Paul at Colchester[3] that there was often an appeal from the court
of the soken to that of the borough. Most of the
sokens mentioned in the list of Edward II's reign
were of post-conquest origin, as they belonged to
certain monastic and collegiate churches which had
been founded after the Conquest, and had received
royal grants that they should exercise sake and soke
over their own men; but notwithstanding these
royal grants, the courts of the sokens were feudal
courts and exercised merely the ordinary jurisdiction that was exercised by the lord of an ordinary
manor over his tenants.

I would suggest that it is in this connection that
we can see the greatest difference between the older
towns of England and those of France; as far back
as we can trace them there were towns in England

---

[1] *B. B. C.* 126.   [2] *B. B. C.* 130.
[3] *B. B. C.* 129.

that had royal or national courts exercising jurisdiction over all the burgesses, while the sokens were encroachments on these royal courts. But, in the oldest stages of many French towns, we find several authorities each administering his own feudal justice over a portion of the town: our argument, as it will be seen, is not affected by the fact that French feudal justice was often more extended and dealt with more important business than English feudal justice. The Bishop and the Count certainly had their portions of a French town ; the King's portion had probably been sub-infeudated to an official, and any monasteries that there may have been in the town exercised justice over those portions that belonged to them ; and possibly the adjoining landowners had some town houses, over which they also exercised justice, but these town houses differed from the English town houses, in that they were not considered as appurtenances of the rural estates, and were not charged with the repair of the walls. In the second half of the eleventh century Amboise was divided between three lords : two of them quarrelled and fought a savage war in the streets of the town, and in the course of the warfare the whole town was burnt to the ground[1] ; at the beginning of the twelfth century Arles was divided into four quarters, all divided by walls from one another and forming

[1] Flach, *Origines de l'ancienne France* II, 352.

as it were four separate towns, and there were six
lords who exercised jurisdiction over these four
quarters[1]. At Amiens there were six authorities,
the count and the bishop, the vidame and the
vicomte, the châtelain and the avoué[2]. And
examples could be multiplied. And when a commune was formed it embraced all the inhabitants
irrespective of the jurisdiction to which they belonged,
and they elected their mayor and échevins who
administered justice to all the members of the
commune, and in some cases were empowered to
make bye-laws for the good government of the
town. This communal court was the only court at
which all the burgesses were justiciable in the same
way as the English burgesses were justiciable at the
court of the hundredal borough ; but the communal
court was formed by encroachments on the courts
of the grandees who owned portions of the town,
whereas in England the court of the hundredal
borough was a national court and the sokens were
the encroachments of the grandees on the national
courts. In many cases, where the King of France
had granted a charter sanctioning or ratifying the
commune, he tried to assume the seignory of that
commune, and to lay down the principle that such communes were held of him[3]: the grandees protested

---

[1] Flach, *Origines de l'ancienne France* II, 274—5.
[2] *Ib.* 297.   [3] Luchaire, *Les Communes Françaises* 270.

against this doctrine and succeeded in their protest[1]; but if the king had succeeded, we should
have seen a royal court formed by encroachments
on the feudal courts, in distinction to the English
custom of forming feudal courts by encroachments
on the royal courts[2].

Possibly this comparison between French and
English municipalities will throw light on another
problem : it is a commonplace that the sworn commune never took root in England; if I am correct in
my explanation of the relationship between the court
of the commune and the seignorial courts, the reason
is clear. From the very earliest times the English
borough had a court at which all the burgesses were
justiciable, to obtain which was one of the objects of
the French commune. True, until the borough was
farmed by the burgesses, the presiding officer of this

[1] Luchaire, *Les Communes Françaises* 272.

[2] In this interpretation of the French evidence, I am in great
part following Professor Ashley's summary of M. Flach's views on
the origin of towns in France (*Surveys Historic and Economic*
178): but I am bound to say that M. Flach does not appear to
consider the case of a commune being formed in a town of
divided authority ; in the two examples that he quotes he suggests
that the commune was directed against a single lord, the Bishop
of Cambrai and the Count of Maine ; and in all fairness to
Messrs Ashley and Flach, I must add that neither of them is
responsible for my views on the relation between the court of the
commune and the seignorial courts.

court was the nominee of the sheriff or of the lord of the borough, but the doomsmen were the offender's fellow burgesses, and not the men of another lord, as might possibly be the case in a French town, and in those English towns where there was a merchant guild, there was a second court which had jurisdiction over all the members of the guild, and was presided over by the elected head of the guild. But Richard of Devises tells us that during the absence of Richard I from England, Prince John, as regent, took an oath to the commune of London on October 8th, 1191[1], and Dr Round has printed the oath of fealty taken by the commune to King Richard during his imprisonment in Germany[2]. What was this commune and what were its functions?

Now, one result of our examination of the English boroughs of the twelfth century and before is the evidence that in the twelfth century the institutions of London were absolutely normal and differed from those of the other boroughs of the kingdom, not in kind but merely in degree; firstly, like so many boroughs, London lay outside the rural hundreds; three rural hundreds of Sussex ran up to the boundaries of the lands belonging to the City of Chichester, and there stopped short; the rural

---

[1] *Select Charters* 252.
[2] *Commune of London* 235—6.

hundred of Ossulton in Middlesex ran up to the boundaries of the lands belonging to the City of London and there stopped short; secondly, Domesday Book and the Pipe Rolls show that except where a borough had been granted in farm to some person or body of persons, the sheriff accounted at the Exchequer for the income arising from the shire and the boroughs within it; Dr Round has shown that the sheriff of Middlesex and the portreeve of London was one and the same person, and that the farm of London and Middlesex was always paid to the Exchequer by one and the same person or body of persons[1]; thirdly, Edgar's law required the burghimot to be held thrice a year; the folkmoot of London was held thrice a year at Michaelmas, Christmas, and Midsummer, and at these three sessions all the citizens attended without special summons[2]: if the folkmoot had been a shiremoot, it would, in accordance with Edgar's law, have been held twice a year[3]; fourthly, in other boroughs, there were more frequent sittings of the borough court which were attended only by those who had received special summons; in London, by the side of the folkmoot, was the weekly husting which was attended only by those who had been specially summoned[4]; fifthly, Domesday Book shows that

---

[1] *Geoffrey de Mandeville* 353, 359.   [2] 17 *E. H. R.* 502.
[3] *Select Charters* 71.   [4] *B. B. C.* 142.

York was divided into six wards and Cambridge into 10; there were 20 wards in London in the reign of Henry I[1] and 24 a century later[2], and both Miss Bateson and M. Petit Dutaillis were of opinion that the aldermen of these wards were the *skivini* mentioned in the oath of fealty[3]; sixthly, like all our old towns, London was divided ecclesiastically into a number of parishes : there were 11 parishes within the walls of the City of Oxford, and Fitz-stephen says there were 136 parish churches in London[4]; seventhly, the charters show that the Bishop of London had a soken at Colchester[5], and the Canons of Grimsby had a soken at Grimsby[6]; there were nine sokens in Stamford in 1086[7]; we can compile a list of about a score of sokens in London in the reign of Edward II[8]; eighthly, the Pipe Roll of 1130 shows that there were then Weavers' Guilds at Oxford, Lincoln and Huntingdon, as well as in London, and there was also a Bakers' Guild in London. The only difference that I can see between London and the other boroughs was that in London there were more wards, more parishes, more sokens,

---

[1] *Hist. Account of Guildhall*, p. 16.   [2] *Ib.* 167.

[3] 17 *E. H. R.* 508, *Studies Supplemental to Stubbs*, 99.

[4] Stow, *Survey of London* (Everyman's Series), 501.

[5] *B. B. C.* 129.   [6] *B. B. C.* 125.

[7] *D. B.* 1, 336 *b* 2 ; *Dom. Bor.* 51.

[8] *Hundred Rolls* 1, 401, 420.

and more guilds than elsewhere. But we must not attribute more governmental functions to the wards and parishes than they actually possessed : one most tempting analogy must be resisted : a rural hundred was composed of many vills : an urban hundred might be divided into many wards ; but the Pipe Rolls show that the urban ward was not the equivalent of the rural vill ; again and again the printed Pipe Rolls record the payment of fines by rural vills for some transgression or another, but they never record the payment of a fine by an urban ward : the wards of London appear to have had four functions and four functions only ; they were entrusted with the assessment and collection of the Royal aids and the rates required for city purposes[1] ; each ward had to find guards for one or another of the city gates ; the ward jury acted as a leet jury and presented nuisances ; and the alderman of each ward was responsible for the administration of the Assize of Arms within his ward, and was the leader of the armed forces of his ward, but such forces were arrayed under the pennon of the parish to which they belonged[2]. It is scarcely necessary to remind you that till the sixteenth century the parish was an ecclesiastical organ and had no civil functions, and that the Tudor Poor and Highway laws first entrusted civil functions to the ecclesiastical organ.

[1] 17 *E. H. R.* 728.   [2] 17 *E. H. R.* 728.

From this digression into the functions of the wards it is clear that any authority that they possessed, they possessed in subordination to the folkmoot, and we have seen that the courts of the sokens were encroachments on the folkmoot, so that it is clear that from the earliest times there was a strong centralised body which could speak and act for the whole city and for all the citizens, and that London always possessed one of the objects which were sought by the French communes. But the folkmoot was under the presidency of the sheriff or sheriffs, who throughout the twelfth century, except for a few years at the end of the reign of Henry I, were the nominees of the king : and what the Londoners sought, and what they obtained, by the establishment of their commune was the right to elect the presiding officer in the person of the mayor : his official position was recognised by Richard on his return from captivity, and was definitely secured by John's charter of 1215 authorising the Londoners to elect a mayor. With this right secured to them, the Londoners had obtained the second object sought by the French communes, and it is not therefore surprising that nothing more is heard of the commune of London.

There are many other towns in which the history of the mayoralty is very similar to that of the mayoralty of London. In the first place we find that a person calling himself mayor of the borough appears as a witness to deeds : it is obvious that he would not be thus styled mayor unless he was recognised as such by his fellow burgesses ; secondly, writs are addressed to him out of the royal chancery, implying the royal recognition of his office ; and finally, sometimes centuries after his first recognition by the King, there is a royal charter authorising the burgesses to elect a mayor. This is the sequence of events at Cambridge, Chester, Chichester, Leicester, Oxford and Salisbury, to name only half a dozen towns, and it is noteworthy that in all these six towns there was a merchant guild before the mayor was first mentioned.

But we have wandered far from our starting point—the difference between feudal and royal justice, and in our discussion of the differences between the court of the seignorial borough and that of the hundredal borough, we have overlooked the element that was common to both. The example of Eynsham has shown us the manner in which a mesne lord would create a borough, by granting all the land within a certain area on burgage tenure, and establishing a session of his manorial court for the control of that area ; but the manorial court was simply a modification of the primeval township moot, a moot, which in its origin was administrative rather than judicial. Now the court of a rural hundred was financial and judicial rather than administrative, and when we find the court of a hundredal borough, an urban hundred, exercising administrative functions, we see that that court contains an element which is wanting in the court of the rural hundred: that element can be attributed to nothing else but the primeval township moot. This is corroborative evidence in support of Stubbs' dictum "the *burh* of the Anglo-Saxon period is simply a more organised form of the township[1]"; and our investigations have shown us that this higher organisation consisted in the super-position of the organisation of the hundred on that of the township. It is, however, permissible to doubt whether all the *burhs* of the Anglo-Saxon period possessed higher organisations than those of the neighbouring rural manors; in the thirteenth century most of the seignorial boroughs had no higher organisation than that of the manors from which they had been amputated; and such seignorial boroughs were valued for purposes of taxation along with the vills of which they had previously formed part. Now Domesday Book shows us some 25 or 30 rural manors containing within their boundaries boroughs which are not valued separately from the manors, and analogy with the seignorial boroughs of the thirteenth century suggests that they were not separately

[1] *Const. Hist.* I, 92.

valued because their organisation was no higher than that of the manors in which they lay.

But although the primitive township is an element in the borough, it must be noticed that the seignorial borough is the result of a definite act of creation on the part of the lord, and that the imposition of the hundredal organisation is also the result of a definite act on the part of the King. Hence, with the possible exception of those Roman towns which became English boroughs and always seem to have lain outside the rural organisation, all our boroughs acquired their distinctive organisation by definite acts of creation.

APPENDIXES

I. THE GARRISON THEORY

THE "garrison theory" does not command general acceptance and it is therefore necessary to discuss briefly the various objections that have been urged against it, and the answers thereto.

In her first criticisms[1] of my *Domesday Boroughs* Miss Bateson maintained that the burgesses mentioned in Domesday Book in connection with rural manors were men who resided in those manors but had burgess rights in the town: in my reply[2], I pointed out that this contention could not account for the houses that were physically situate in the boroughs, and paid rent to rural manors, and that there was evidence for believing that the Domesday scribes spoke of the houses or the burgesses as fancy moved them. She then[3] began her rejoinder in these words: "In my review of Mr Ballard's Domesday Boroughs it was not my intention to suggest that every burgess who paid rent to a manor resided on that manor and had no house in any town. My plea

[1] 20 *E. H. R.* 149.   [2] 21 *E. H. R.* 699.
[3] 21 *E. H. R.* 709.

throughout was for variety in the explanations advanced to account for the association between town houses and rural properties, and while admitting the possibility that some burgesses may have acquitted rural estates of burghal service, my protest was made against that theory as incapable of explaining the whole of the evidence." But if she admits the theory in some cases, who is to decide the cases to which it is not applicable? I must emphasise this point for when M. Petit Dutaillis wrote his Appendixes to Stubbs' *Constitutional History*, since translated as *Studies Supplemental to Stubbs*, he had not seen my reply to Miss Bateson nor her rejoinder.

Three other objections to the theory can best be put in the shape of question and answer: How comes it that Domesday records town houses which are appurtenant to manors that are not situate in the same county as the borough? There are only a few boroughs to which this question applies: London, Tamworth and Wallingford were border towns and were not unnaturally fortified by their adjoining counties: Oxford is also a border town, and contained houses paying rents to Steventon in Berks and to two manors in Bucks: and Mr Round has shown that four of the manors recorded in the Hereford Domesday as having houses in Worcester, were really situate in Worcestershire, and that there was only one Herefordshire manor which had houses in the city of Worcester.

Is it not possible, in view of the pre-conquest laws forbidding extra-urban traffic, and the burgesses' monopoly of trade within their boroughs, that the resident burgesses who paid rent to rural manors resided in the boroughs as the accredited agents of their fellow villagers for trading purposes? But the gildsman's monopoly of sale was generally suspended during fairs and in some places on market days[1], and on these days the villagers could visit the towns and do their trafficking on payment of the usual tolls : so that there was no necessity for the residence of permanent agents. Moreover, it is doubtful whether some of the villages which had appurtenant town houses had sufficient surplus produce for sale to require a resident agent in a town : there were two houses in Leicester pertaining to Desford, a vill of four carucates occupied by only one villain with one team[2]. Can it be contended that this one farmer required two salesmen in Leicester ?

Why is it impossible to establish a proportion between the number of burgesses or town houses possessed by a manor and the extent or assessment of that manor ? The statistics of Dunwich and Wallingford answer that question ; in each town the rural landowners held "acres," and it would naturally be to their advantage to crowd as many houses as possible on these individual acres to secure larger rents : at Wallingford Milo Crispin had one acre belonging to Sutton on which were six houses and another belonging to Bray on which were eleven houses.

Another objection is that of M. Petit Dutaillis who points out that heterogeneity of tenure was known on the continent : the French and German towns were "nothing but juxtapositions of patchwork, of fragments of great estates ; there is no reason for attributing an absolutely original growth to English towns[3]" : it must be admitted that there was much tenurial heterogeneity in continental towns, but according to the evidence at our disposal the

---

[1] *Gild Merchant* I, 47.   [2] *D. B.* I, 230 *a* I, 232 *a* I.
[3] *Studies Supplemental to Stubbs* 82.

heterogeneity of continental towns differed from that of England, inasmuch as on the continent the town houses belonging to others than the lord of the town were not considered as being appurtenant to nor were they conveyed along with the rural manors of the magnates. Nor again, do I know any evidence that in France the duty of repairing the walls of the towns was charged on the rural landowners: in other words, burhbot was unknown in France. So that continental conditions differed entirely from those of England, and we cannot employ the argument from analogy.

Professor Tait[1] suggests that the rents payable to rural manors in respect of burgesses in towns may represent payments for permission to live away from the manor, like the chivagium of later days: but this suggestion fails in that it does not explain how the payments came to be attached to houses; nor does it explain why the payments were, with a few exceptions, from the houses or inhabitants of a town to the manors of the county in which it was situate or the adjoining counties: London contained houses and burgesses paying rents to manors in Surrey and Essex: does any one dare say that the only immigrants into London came from Surrey and Essex?

Finally, let me point out a remarkable analogy: the supporters of the garrison theory contend that some of the rural landowners performed their burhbot by keeping houses in the boroughs and burgesses in those houses; three years ago I called attention to the fact that some of the grandees who owed castle guard to the castles of Newcastle-on-Tyne, Bamburgh and Dover were bound by their tenure to maintain

[1] 12 *E. H. R.* 775.

houses within those castles where their knights might reside during their term of duty[1]. Since then I have found that the same custom existed in connection with the castle of Durham[2]; and there is evidence which suggests that it was also to be found at Alnwick[3]. These instances throw light on the statements in Domesday Book that Roger had two masures in the castle of Ewias[4] and Osbern had 23 men in the castle of Auretone[5]; and suggest that the King and some barons, when they founded their castles and enfeoffed knights to hold by the service of castle guard, followed the example of Alfred, and gave to these knights, houses within the walls of the castle where their men might reside when they were required to perform their service.

II. THE ROMAN BOROUGHS

No one knows the exact number of towns that were inhabited during the Roman occupation of England: we are told of colonies at Colchester, London, Lincoln and York, and it is believed that Verulamium was a municipium[6]: but although there were few Roman towns which obtained municipal institutions, there were many settlements, larger than mere villages and surrounded with walls. Till the Legions were withdrawn they all enjoyed a greater or less degree of cultured life, and even after the withdrawal of the Legions, whatever culture there was in the country

---

[1] 24 *E. H. R.* 712.

[2] *Feodarium Prioratus Dunelmensis* 196 n.

[3] *Percy Cartulary*, cp. p. 371 with p. 456.

[4] *D. B.* 1, 185 *a* 2.   [5] *D. B.* 1, 186 *b* 2.

[6] *Studies Supplemental to Stubbs* 72.

was to be found in the towns. Calleva Atrebatorum was inhabited till into the sixth century, but was evacuated at the approach of the Germanic invaders and has never since been inhabited[1]. According to the Chronicle, Anderida was burnt, but although the houses within the walls were burnt and the inhabitants massacred, the Roman walls remain to this day. There is no evidence that the invaders deliberately destroyed the Roman towns; they left them severely alone as the work of giants and the home of ghosts, and settled at their gates. Even to-day the walls of Richborough, Pevensey and Burgh Castle impress the most casual observer: what then must have been the impression that they made on the ignorant and superstitious savage from over the sea. One of their poets has preserved his thoughts at the sight of the deserted city of Bath in the poem called The Ruin.

One result of the superstition of the invaders and their consequent avoidance of the old Roman towns and the extramural territories on which their dead were buried, is the fact that the rural hundreds come up to their boundaries and there stop short. On the east and west of the Roman walls of Anderida, the Saxons fixed their settlements of East and West Ham, but the fortified area lay outside both townships. The Domesday hundreds of Box, Stockbridge and Singleton embrace the city of Chichester, and its extramural lands, and three rural hundreds come up to the boundaries of the extramural lands of the Roman town of Leicester, but both Chichester and Leicester lie outside the rural hundreds. Sir Laurence Gomme attributes the non-inclusion of London in the rural hundreds of Middlesex

---

[1] *Studies Supplemental to Stubbs* 73.

to the military strength of the surviving inhabitants: but, whatever may be the reason, the exclusion of some of the old Roman towns from the rural hundreds is a fact of the highest importance; and of the 20 Roman towns that were styled boroughs in Domesday Book, 16 lay outside the rural hundreds and only four, St Albans, Bath, Dunwich and Ilchester, appear to have been grouped with rural vills to form hundreds of the ordinary type, and Bath, Dunwich and Ilchester were all separately mentioned in the *Nomina Villarum*, a fact which shows that they were hundredal boroughs in the fourteenth century.

The year 410 is generally accepted as the date of the withdrawal of the Legions: in 597 St Augustine landed in Kent, and, according to Bede[1], his first gift from the King was a piece of land in Canterbury. In 604 Augustine consecrated Bishops to live in the old Roman towns of Rochester and London[2]: in 627 Paulinus and Felix were respectively consecrated Bishops of York and Dunwich[3]; and in the following year the reeve of Lincoln was converted and a Bishop consecrated in that city[4]; in 635 Birinus was consecrated Bishop of Dorchester, Oxon[5], and in 643 a new see was established at Winchester: the first Bishop whose see was fixed at any but an old Roman town was the Bishop of the Mercians whose see was fixed at Repton in 653[6] and afterwards removed to Lichfield. So that the first eight bishops in England were established in old Roman towns, a fact which shows that during the

---

[1] Bede, *Ecc. Hist.* Bk I, c. 26.
[2] *Ib.* Bk II, c. 3.
[3] *Ib.* c. 15.
[4] *Ib.* c. 16.
[5] *Ib.* Bk III, c. 7.
[6] *Ib.* c. 21.

troublous times of the English invasions, there was material persistence of these old towns. Sir Laurence Gomme maintains that, in addition to this material persistence, Roman municipal institutions and Roman private law persisted in London till its surrender to Edward the Elder in 912[1]: but the evidence adduced in support of this position is not very convincing.

Further evidence of the persistence of the old Roman towns is to be found in the fact that our kings, prior to Alfred, had mints only at Canterbury, London, Lincoln and York, all four of Roman foundation: Alfred's coins come from these four and from four other towns of Roman origin, Bath, Exeter, Gloucester and Winchester; Athelstan was the first king to coin in any town not of Roman foundation[2].

If the traditions embodied in the English Chronicle are to be trusted, the old Roman towns played no part in the battles of kites and crows as Milton styled the struggles between the various kingdoms of the Heptarchy; but with the beginnings of the Danish raids, their use as fortified refuges begins to be recognised: for in 814[3] the King of Mercia gave a house in Canterbury "ad refugium necessitatis," for a refuge in case of necessity, to the Abbess of Lyminge, whose nunnery lay on the seacoast near Hythe. The walls of these refuges would be repaired by the rural landowners under the trinoda necessitas, but although the teaching of Christianity probably broke down much of the superstition of the Anglo-Saxons, yet it is certain that the intramural spaces were very sparsely inhabited. Nehemiah was faced with the same problem when he had rebuilt the

---

[1] *The Making of London* 90. [2] *Supra*, p. 43.
[3] *Domesday Boroughs* 107.

walls of Jerusalem ; like the Anglo-Saxon, the Jew of that day preferred village to town life : and while some volunteered to live in Jerusalem " the rest of the people cast lots to bring one of ten to dwell in Jerusalem, the holy city, and nine parts to dwell in the other cities[1]." Alfred dealt with this problem in another way, and to secure the restoration of London granted two several acres of land within the city to the Archbishop of Canterbury and the Bishop of Worcester respectively[2], who were doubtless required to build houses on these acres and to find burgesses to dwell in these houses. The example, once set, would seem to have been generally followed, with the result that of the 20 Roman towns styled boroughs in Domesday Book, there is only one—St Albans—which did not then contain houses or burgesses paying rent to rural manors : but a deed of 996 shows that the manors of Byrston and Wincelfield had nine appurtenant houses in St Albans[3] so that in the tenth century all the Roman boroughs were of heterogeneous tenure.

We have already seen evidence that the composite boroughs were fortified ; and it therefore appears that all the Roman towns which became English boroughs were fortified during the tenth century, and it has been noticed that 16 out of the 20 lay outside the rural hundreds.

This evidence from the Roman boroughs supports our previous argument that there was some connection between tenurial heterogeneity and extra-hundredality : but this connection first appears in the Roman boroughs, using

[1] Nehemiah xi. 1.
[2] *Domesday Book and Beyond* 189 n.
[3] Kemble, No. 696.

this term to signify those Roman towns which became English boroughs, and it would seem to follow that when the new boroughs were fortified, Edward the Elder and his successors followed the example which had been set in connection with the old Roman towns, and gave them a court of their own equivalent to the courts of the rural hundreds.

The evidence from the Roman boroughs may be summed up as follows : the old Roman towns were deserted after the Saxon invasions and owed their re-settlement to the work and influence of the Christian missionaries : from very early times they were treated apart from the rural organisation of the shire, with the result that they were regarded as urban hundreds having courts of their own : their walls were repaired by the rural landowners under the trinoda necessitas, and served as defences against the Danish raiders : but they were still sparsely populated and to secure a population Alfred gave plots of land within their walls to some of the rural land-owners who owed burhbot, on which they built houses and kept burgesses : then, when Edward the Elder fortified certain Midland boroughs, he obtained a population for them in the same way as Alfred had peopled the Roman boroughs of Wessex, and the boroughs thus created were treated as urban hundreds in the same way as the older Roman boroughs.

III. THE "LIBER BURGUS"

In my *British Borough Charters*[1] it was said that the idea of the "liber burgus" seems to have been the only idea added to municipal jurisprudence during the reign of King John: the term was in constant use after that date but no definition of its meaning is known to me: in a plea of 1350 the burgesses of Macclesfield pleaded "that by the words 'quod villa de Maclesfeld sit liber burgus' they claim that the same town shall be a liber burgus, and shall have all the liberties and customs which a liber burgus ought to have[2]." But this is no definition; and we must therefore try to ascertain the effect of this grant.

I have been unable to find any difference between a borough and a free borough: the two requisites for a borough were burgage tenure for all its tenements and a court with jurisdiction over all its inhabitants, except the inhabitants of sokens, and I cannot find that there was any additional requisite for the formation of a "free borough," and would therefore suggest that the term was introduced by the lawyers of John's reign to shorten the verbiage of charters.

It must, however, be noticed that there were two kinds of free boroughs varying according to the competence of the grantor of the charter: if a mesne lord created a free borough, the only court he would be able to establish would be a manorial court, where he would exercise over his tenants the rights defined by the term "sake and soke": if the King created a free borough he would create a

---

[1] p. xv. [2] *Gild Merchant* II, 171.

hundredal court for the borough, and by so doing would exempt the burgesses from the jurisdiction of the rural hundred in which the borough was geographically situate, and would impose on them the duty of sending twelve representatives to the Eyre, and also representatives to Parliament. This distinction is clearly shown in Dorset; in 1284 the King granted a charter conferring on Lyme the status of a free borough; and Lyme appears in the *Nomina Villarum* as a borough, and therefore presumably was entitled to separate representation at the Eyre and in Parliament. In 1254 the Prior of Winchester created a free borough at Weymouth, but Weymouth does not appear in the *Nomina Villarum*.

With the grant of a separate court came the privileges implied by the possession of that court, the right to compound offences as at Norham[1], and the right to elect twelve capital portmen, as at Ipswich[2]: but neither the "firma burgi" nor the merchant guild were appurtenances of the "liber burgus[3]."

It is, however, from the litigation which resulted in the cancellation of a charter granted to the burgesses of Wells by Edward III in 1341, that incidentally we learn most about the nature of the "liber burgus[4]." Domesday Book speaks of Wells as a rural manor only[5] but Richard, Bishop of Wells (1135—66), cut out of his manor an area with defined boundaries, which he created a borough, in the same way as, in the next century, the Abbot of Eynsham

---

[1] *B. B. C.* 112.   [2] *Gild Merchant* II, 119.

[3] *Ib.* I, 89.

[4] *Year Book*, 16 Edw. III, part 1, Introd. pp. xxiv—xciv (Rolls Series).   [5] *D. B.* I, 89 *a* 2.

created a borough at Eynsham: his charter is lost but was confirmed by his two successors, who gave the burgesses the monopoly of sale of hides and leather and certain rights at certain fairs; but the court of this borough was merely a manorial court. However, in 1201, King John conferred the status of a "liber burgus" on this manorial borough of Wells; we have argued that by this grant he exempted the burgesses from suit of the court of the rural hundred and conferred on the court of the borough the status of a hundredal court: and in corroboration of this position it is to be noted that in an Inquisition connected with the litigation, it is stated that the Bishop had a Hundred Court in and for the vill of Wells[1]; and, in the early part of the fourteenth century we find that Wells is returned in the *Nomina Villarum* as a borough, that it sent burgesses to Parliament during the reigns of Edward I and II, and paid the sixth of 1322, all points of evidence that it was a hundredal borough.

In 1341, the burgesses obtained a new charter from Edward III granting them (1) freedom from toll throughout England, (2) the right to elect a Mayor, Bailiffs and Constables, (3) the right to elect a Coroner to keep the pleas of the Crown, (4) the right to keep a gaol, (5) the return of all writs: (6) they were not to plead or be impleaded without the borough, nor (7) to be placed on juries with men from outside the borough, and (8) they were allowed to fortify their town[2]. But the fatal point in connection with this charter was that it had not been preceded by an "Inquisitio ad quod damnum," an inquisition which, by this time, was a condition precedent to any new charter.

---

[1] *Y. B.* 16 Edw. III, pt. 1, p. lxii.   [2] *Ib.* xlix.

Consequently, steps were taken for the revocation of the charter; the litigation was very long and technical; it was alleged that many of these privileges would be to the damage of the King, inasmuch as, being damage to the Bishop, the King would lose profits which he would otherwise receive during the vacancy of the see.

Eventually it was held that the omission of the " Inquisitio ad quod damnum" vitiated the grant of the charter, and the burgesses were ordered to deliver it to the Chancery for cancellation. But, for our purpose, it is important to note, that the burgesses did not use the grant of the "liber burgus" as evidence that they were in possession of any of these privileges before the grant of the new charter: if any of them could have been claimed as being implied by the "liber burgus," it is certain that the burgesses would have relied on that grant, especially as John's charter had been inspected and confirmed by Edward I in 1290.

The record of this litigation throws light on another point: it will be remembered that the burgesses of Ipswich elected 12 capital portmen "as there are in the other 'liberi burgi' in England[1]": during the Wells litigation it was certified to the King that " Twelve burgesses and the rest of the community had the keeping (*custodiam*) of the town for a certain number of years, in virtue of an indenture made between them and the Bishop, for which, and for the profits issuing out of the town, they paid the Bishop 100 marks sterling per annum[2]." Were these 12 burgesses of Wells the doomsmen of the hundred court of the borough and possibly its permanent delegation to the Eyre?

[1] *Gild Merchant* II, 119.   [2] *Y. B.* u. s. lxviii.

IV. LONDON

It might be contended that the institutions of London were abnormal for the few years during the twelfth century when the citizens elected a sheriff or sheriffs who collected the joint farm of the city of London and the County of Middlesex, and accounted for it at the Exchequer; but this abnormality existed only at two periods; first, from the granting of the Charter of Henry I, in 1130 or 1131, till Stephen's grant of the shrievalty of London and Middlesex to Geoffrey de Mandeville at Christmas 1141[1], and secondly from the 5th day of July 1199, when John granted the shrievalty of London and Middlesex to the citizens of London for £300 a year[2]: so that for seven-eighths of the century, the sheriffs of London and Middlesex were the nominees of the King[3], in the same way as the sheriffs of the other shires were likewise nominees of the King. But the duties of the sheriffs were well defined; they collected the dues accruing to the King from the county and accounted for them at the Exchequer; they had the return of all writs within the shire (except where the lord or the inhabitants of a district had this privilege), and they executed all judicial process: but neither the sheriffs nor the citizens of London exercised any governmental functions over Middlesex, and certainly never treated it as a "subject district." The Custumals of the City—the Liber Albus, the Liber Custumarum, the Liber de Antiquis legibus, and the Anonymous Collection printed by Miss Bateson in the *English Historical Review*—are full of

[1] *Geoffrey de Mandeville* 141.   [2] *B. B. C.* 220.
[3] *Geoffrey de Mandeville* 372, especially lines 21, 22.

regulations dealing with persons and property within the walls, but they contain no regulations relating to any persons or property in any of the villages of Middlesex.

But, even if it be granted that for ten or twelve years during the twelfth century, the King's representatives within the City of London were abnormal in that they exercised certain restricted functions in the County of Middlesex, yet that is the extent of the abnormality, and with that exception, as is contended in the lecture, "the institutions of London differed from those of the other boroughs in the Kingdom not in kind, but only in degree," and examination of those institutions does not bear out Bishop Stubbs when he speaks of "their (i.e. the Londoners') shire organisation under the sheriff[1]." If London had been organised as a shire, its folkmoot would have been a shire-moot and, according to Edgar's law, have been held twice a year, whereas our earliest information shows us the folkmoot meeting thrice a year[2], as was ordered by Edgar of the Burghimot, and was the rule at Whitby[3].

Dr Round quotes, with approval, another dictum of Stubbs that London was only "a bundle of communities townships parishes and lordships of which each had its own institutions[4]," but he disagrees with Stubbs' suggestion that this complicated organisation was displaced by a shire organisation, and in his turn suggests that "the sheriff and the folkmoot could no more bind these self-governing bodies into one coherent whole, than they could or did in the case of an ordinary shire....But what the sheriff and

---

[1] *Sel. Ch.* 107, 5th Edit.
[2] 17 *E. H. R.* 502.
[3] *B. B. C.* 142.
[4] *Const. Hist.* I, 404, qu. *Geoffrey de Mandeville* 356.

folkmoot could not accomplish, the mayor and commune could and did[1]."

But Dr Round himself has produced evidence that more than half a century before the appearance of the first Mayor of London, the citizens acted as a "coherent whole" when they claimed that they were entitled to elect the King, and made a treaty with Stephen before they proceeded to elect him as King[2]; three or four years later they sent a deputation on behalf of their "communio" to the Council at Winchester by which the Empress was elected to be lady of England[3]. At this date the folkmoot was the only body of which we have any knowledge, to which all the citizens owed suit, and therefore it alone could speak on their behalf. But Stephen was not the only King in whose election the Londoners took part; they elected Edmund Ironsides in 1015[4], and after the Battle of Hastings, they, with the Archbishop of York and earls Edwin and Morcar, elected Edgar Atheling as Harold's successor[5]. There is no definite evidence of communal action at these last two elections and it may have been that the citizens played merely the part of the shouting crowd, the part that was played by the boys of Westminster school at the last two coronations. But there are other passages in which Dr Round treats the Londoners as acting as a "coherent whole," even before 1191, when he deals with the charter of Henry I and their transactions in respect of the farm of London and Middlesex[6]: analogy with other boroughs suggests that it was the folkmoot that carried on these negotiations[7].

[1] *Geoffrey de Mandeville* 357.   [2] *Ib.* 2, 247.
[3] Stubbs, *Const. Hist.* I, 407.   [4] *Norm. Conq.* I, 397.
[5] *Ib.* III, 524.   [6] *Geoffrey de Mandeville* 363.   [7] *B.B.C.* cii.

Table showing the characteristics of certain Domesday Boroughs.

		Roman origin	Burghal Hidage	Edward the Elder	Preconquest Mint	DOMESDAY Hundred	Composite	Third Penny
		1	2	3	4	5	6	7
1	Arundel					Extra	H B	
2	Axbridge							T. P.
3	Barnstaple		B. H.				H B	T. P.
4	Bath	R	B. H.		M		H B	T. P.
5	Bedford				M	Extra		(T. P.)
6	Bristol				M		H	?
7	Bridport		?			Extra	A	
8	Bruton				M		B	T. P.
9	Buckingham		B. H.	E. E.	M	Extra	B	
10	Calne						H B	
11	Cambridge				M	Extra	H B	(T. P.)
12	Canterbury	R			M	Extra	H B	
13	Chester	R		E. E.	M	Extra	H B	T. P.
14	Chichester	R	B. H.		M	Extra	H B	T. P.
15	Colchester	R			M	Extra	H	
16	Cricklade		B. H.		M	Extra	H B	T. P.
17	Derby				M	Extra	H	T. P.
18	Dorchester	R			M	Extra	H B	
19	Dover	R			M	Extra	H	T. P.
20	Droitwich						H B	T. P.
21	Dunwich	R				Intra	A B	
22	Exeter	R	B. H.		M	Extra	H	T. P.
23	Fordwich					Own		T. P.
24	Frome							T. P.
25	Gloucester	R			M	Extra	H B	
26	Grantham					Extra	H	
27	Guildford				M	Intra	H	
28	Hastings		B. H.		M		B	
29	Hereford				M	Extra	B	T. P.
30	Hertford			E. E.	M	Extra	H	
31	Huntingdon			E. E.	M	Extra	H B	T. P.
32	Hythe				M	Intra	B	
33	Ilchester	R			M		B	T. P.
34	Ipswich				M	Own	H B	T. P.
35	Langport		B. H.		M		H B	T. P.
36	Leicester	R			M	Extra	H B	T. P.
37	Lewes		B. H.		M	Extra	H B	T. P.
38	Lincoln	R			M	Extra	H B	T. P.
39	London	R			M	(Extra)	H B	
40	Maldon			E. E.	M	Own	B	

Table showing the characteristics of certain
Domesday Boroughs, continued.

		Roman origin	Burghal Hidage	Edward the Elder	Preconquest Mint	DOMESDAY				
						Hundred	Composite			Third Penny
		1	2	3	4	5	6			7
41	Malmesbury		B. H.		M	Extra	H	A	B	T. P.
42	Marlborough									T. P.
43	Milborne								B	T. P.
44	Northampton					Extra	H			
45	Norwich				M	Own	H		B	T. P.
46	Nottingham				M	Extra	H			
47	Oxford		B. H.		M	Extra	H		B	T. P.
48	Pevensey	R				Extra			B	
49	Rochester	R			M	Own	H			
50	Romney				M	Intra			B	
51	Sandwich				M	Own	H			T. P.[1]
52	Salisbury									T. P.
53	Shaftesbury		B. H.		M	Extra			B	
54	Shrewsbury				M	Extra	H		B	T. P.
55	Southampton		B. H.		M	Extra	H			
56	Southwark		B. H.		M	Extra	H			T. P.
57	Stafford			E. E.	M	Extra	H		B	T. P.
58	Stamford				M	Extra	H			
59	Sudbury				M	Intra			B	
60	Tamworth			E. E.	M				B	
61	Thetford				M	Own	H			T. P.
62	Torksey				M	Extra				T. P.
63	Totnes				M					T. P.
64	Wallingford		B. H.		M	Extra	H	A		
65	Warwick		(App.)	E. E.	M	Extra	H		B	
66	Wareham		B. H.		M	Extra	H		B	
67	Wilton		B. H.		M		H		B	
68	Wimbourne						H			
69	Winchcombe				M	Extra			B	T. P.
70	Winchester	R	B. H.		M	(Extra)	H		B	
71	Worcester	R	(App.)	E. E.	M	Extra	H		B	T. P.
72	Yarmouth					Intra				T. P.
73	York	R			M	Extra	H			

NOTES. In column 6, the letters H. A. B. respectively indicate whether the appurtenances of the rural manors are styled Houses, Acres or Burgesses.

From this list are omitted Reading and Twineham (Christchurch) which were included in the list of composite boroughs on pp. 39, 40, of my *Domesday Boroughs*: these two boroughs contained houses paying rent to the lord of the borough and houses paying rent to the church of the town : but it is obvious that the latter class stand in a different category from those paying rent to the lords of rural manors in the neighbourhood

[1] *B. B. C.* 232.

INDEX

Lightning Source UK Ltd.
Milton Keynes UK
UKHW011539180221
378987UK00001B/48